LEADERSHIP
MAXIMS

12 Timeless Leadership Truths

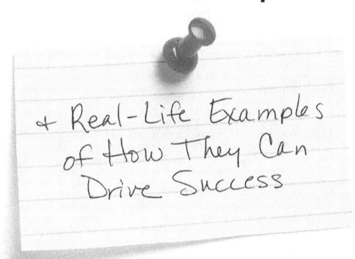

+ Real-Life Examples of How They Can Drive Success

WOODY HESTER

ISBN 978-1-63630-592-9 (Paperback)
ISBN 978-1-63630-593-6 (Hardcover)
ISBN 978-1-63630-594-3 (Digital)

Covenant Books, Inc.
11661 Hwy 707
Murrells Inlet, SC 29576
www.covenantbooks.com

Contents

Foreword

By Kevin Purcell
Senior Director of Organization Development,
Microsoft Corporation, 1994-2004 (Retired); Adjunct
Faculty, College of Business, University of Illinois-
Springfield, Illinois 2007-2019 (Retired)

Leaders operate in a world of complexity and responsibility with challenges coming at them from all directions. To make sense of this world, it is vital to have clarity when addressing those challenges. Leadership Maxims is an incisive book filled with wise leadership maxims and accompanying stories that illustrate their importance.

I met Woody Hester in 2008. He was Chief People Officer of an Award-winning Healthcare System in the Midwest. I worked for and with him as System Director of Organization and Leadership Development. Woody is truly one of the very few "servant leaders" I have ever met. He lives the values of service to others. My work with Woody was to build the foundation of what is today a world-class Leadership Development Institute. Everything I witnessed Woody do was in service of others leadership effectiveness. I quickly noticed how little time he spent in his office. We would often hold our 1-1 meetings either in my office or as we walked around the hospital together. I also noticed that Woody knew the names of almost every-one we would meet in the hallways. Partly because of his having worked there so long (30 years when I knew him) but mainly because he VALUED people so much it was vital to him to know their names. He literally, "lead others by walking around".

I invite you to read this book. I intend to send it to my leader-ship development clients around the world. I am doing this because it is honest, borne of experience, and written by a leader of integrity. Also, I am sure it will help these leaders. Leaders are always itching to find solutions that help them reduce the complexity and complications they face every day. Leaders learn best when the message is delivered with clarity and simplicity. However, it is vital to never water down the message. In honor of this fine book, and the clarity of the stories told, I want to close with a quote by Albert Einstein:" All good ideas should be made as simple as possible, but no simpler". This book, Leadership Maxims, is easy to read and contains lifetime lessons in practical leadership.

Acknowledgments

This work is offered with great humility. All that I know about leadership I learned from others. Those who led me, those I was privileged to lead, and great leaders of the past. I dedicate this work to them. I am most grateful to those who challenged me when I needed to be challenged. It is from them that I learned the most.

I also dedicate this work to my family. Thank you to my wife, Lou, for signing on to the journey and for giving me pointers along the way. Thanks to my children—Jon, Jason, Josh, and Jessica—for becoming extraordinary role models for me as they have grown up and become successful leaders in their own lives.

Finally, I also dedicate this work to you, the reader. No matter what you do in your professional life, may your work with others result in good deeds, and may you and those around you have a positive impact on the human condition. My greatest hope is that these few pages will be of some help to you in that endeavor.

How to Read This Book

Of course, I want you to read it all, but I respectfully suggest that you not read it straight through. Instead, consider reading about just one of the maxims each week. Think of it as a twelve-week course. In fact, consider doing this together with a group of colleagues*.

At the conclusion of each reading, chew on the maxim presented and reflect on the story as you go about your daily life. Consider experiences in your own life where the maxim you are considering came into play, or examples where it didn't, but if it had, it would have made a difference.

Discuss your thinking with others, perhaps your colleague group if it helps you; and when you have mulled it over sufficiently, if it really resonates with you, put it on your "wall" and remember it. Incorporate it into your behavior, and when the circumstances around you speak to it, apply it.

Do the same thing again with the next maxim, and then the next, until you finish the book.

*Visit TimelessLeadershipTruths.com to download a free group discussion guide.

Introduction

In 1970, at the age of twenty-four, I held the rank of captain in the US Army. I had recently returned from a one-year tour of duty in Vietnam, and I was assigned to a staff position at the US Army Air Defense Board at Fort Bliss, Texas. It was a staff job, and I was grateful to have it. A break from the rigors of field duty and the stress of living in a combat environment was very welcome. But it was my first staff job. It would be the first time in my life that I would manage the administrative side of project work and lead a diverse group of people in work that was more intellectual than operational. I felt totally unprepared for the job. The team I was to lead consisted of uniformed staff and Department of the Army Civilians. Schedules were tight, deadlines were absolute, and millions of dollars were at stake. I didn't have time to study leadership theory. I needed pragmatic, practical wisdom that works.

The Air Defense Board's job was to develop requests for proposal for new or improved air defense weapon systems, release them to weapons manufacturers, select finalists, test prototype systems, and ultimately, with appropriate review and approval from higher authority, release contracts for production and sale to the US Army. The members of the prototype test team I was assigned to lead had years of tenure and experience, but as a senior company grade commissioned officer, I was in charge of assigned projects. As grateful as I was to be in a staff position, I was totally without significant experience in this kind of work.

The desk I was assigned to when I arrived was next to the wall in a big room full of other desks. Some of the people in the area around me were on my team, but many weren't. They were members of other teams working on other projects. A small bulletin board was attached to the wall over my desk, and it had nothing on it except a water stain from where condensation had run down the wall. To cover up the stain, I put a few of my favorite quotes on it along with some others I clipped out of trade magazines. One of the quotes was "No matter what you've accomplished, somebody helped you." What I didn't know was that particular timeless truth, the bulletin board itself, and later additions of other timeless truths to that bulletin board, would have a profound impact on my work at the Air Defense Board as well as on the trajectory of my professional life for the next four decades.

In the pages that follow, I want to share twelve of the timeless truths that found their way to that bulletin board, and I want to tell you the real-life stories that proved them to be right. I firmly believe that this simple but powerful wisdom will help you as much as it helped me.

1

MAXIM

No matter what you've accomplished, somebody helped you.
—Althea Gibson

Shortly after my arrival at the Air Defense Board, my team received its first assignment under my leadership. We were to evaluate three competing prototype aerial target systems developed by different manufacturers and select the manufacturer that would be awarded the production contract. Other than the standard testing guidelines provided to me, I barely knew how to start.

I had spent the first several days getting to know my team, and with one exception, they all seemed like competent and helpful people. One of them, however, was a crusty old senior warrant officer who made it clear to me that he had little use for young test officers like me. I was afraid he wasn't going to be much help, and his role, and that of his team's, was critical to the work.

As I sat at my desk pondering this challenge, my eyes fell across that bulletin board and that single random quote, "No matter what you've accomplished, somebody helped you," and it all became clear to me. If this project would be a success, it would be because those on my team, with knowledge and experience, would make it a success. Our ultimate success didn't depend on me as much as it depended on them. They needed to want it to be successful, they needed to own it, and for that matter, they needed to want me to be successful too. I had leadership responsibility for the project. I was the one that was accountable to the division chief, but I couldn't do a thing by myself.

I really needed their help, and that included the help of the crusty senior warrant officer.

By this time, a test officer on another team, whom I often ate lunch with, had added some more quotes from a leadership journal to the bulletin board. One of them was "If you can manage relationships, you can manage anything." As I considered that one, it clearly applied to my circumstance too. While I had gotten to know the members of my team, we were really just acquainted. I knew I needed to know them better. They needed to know me too, and in a professionally appropriate way, we needed to care about each other and what we were doing together. So I rolled up my sleeves and set about the important task of building relationships. I focused on the tough warrant officer a lot because I knew he'd be the hardest to reach and he held a key position. I also spent a lot of one-on-one time with each of the others. I asked questions about their professional past, their experiences, and I asked them for advice. Most important, I asked them for their help. I didn't try to hide the fact that I was inexperienced and needed their help. I was honest and open about that. When I asked the crusty old warrant officer for his help, he laughed and said, "No test officer has ever asked me for help before." Then after an awkward pause, he said, "Will you listen to me and let me do things my way?"

To that I said, "I have to lead this project, and I'm accountable to the division chief, but if you mean will I allow you to lead all of us in those things that are the responsibility of your position on the team, and will I value your guidance about aspects of our work not in my experience, the answer is yes. I just ask that you teach us along the way and that you keep me informed."

He sat back in his chair and said, "Okay, Captain, let's give it a try."

In that moment, I knew it was going to work. I shook his hand and said, "Thank you!"

The end of the US Army Air Defense Board story is that the project was a raving success. The crusty senior warrant officer and I became good friends, our team wound up improving the end product, and the US Army used the selected aerial target system for many years. The big lesson for me was that my team did it; I didn't. All I did was build relationships and credibility with very capable members of the team. Not credibility for what I knew so much as credibility that came from sharing freely what I didn't know. I asked them for their help, and I led with humility. Together, we created the winning chemistry that drove our team's success. *My name was on the final report, but everyone on my team, including that crusty old senior warrant officer, helped me. It was really the team that deserved the credit, not me. I made sure they knew that I knew that, and I celebrated their accomplishment, not mine.*

When I left the Air Defense Board because I was being discharged from the army, that crusty old senior warrant officer came to my send-off reception. Our team's long-tenured administrative assistant told me he'd never come to one of those before. For me, that was almost as gratifying as our project's success.

As I left the US Army Air Defense Board and the army, I cleared my desk and collected my personal belongings. I looked over my bulletin board and reflected on the importance it had played. I was so grateful for that water stain. In that moment, I promised myself that I would never forget the things on the board that had helped me. I knew their importance wasn't limited to my experience at the US Army Air Defense Board. I knew they would continue to be important in every future circumstance involving people. I needed to carry them with me forever. Unwilling to rely on my memory, I carefully removed all of the quotes and ideas from the board and put them in a large envelope. They would eventually be placed on other boards, in other offices, wherever I worked with people. Other bits of wisdom would be added along the way, and for the rest of my professional life, the bulletin board and its contents continued to be my most important leadership tool. I read and reread the things on it over and over again. They became part of me. Whenever I was faced with a circumstance or an event one of them applied to, it jumped into my head and provided me with priceless, practical guidance. They became a sort of instruction manual that was unique to me, my life, my work, and the people I worked with.

For the five years that followed my discharge, thanks to the GI Bill and my wonderful wife, Lou, who assumed responsibility for running our household and taking care of our children, I became a civilian again and immersed myself in full-time formal education and part-time work. I had no office and no bulletin board, but I didn't forget the dozen or so things that were now in the envelope. On occasion, I would get them out and reread them. I began to think of them as leadership and life "maxims." A maxim is defined as "a short statement expressing a general truth or rule of conduct." I applied them in every aspect of my life, whether I was on the job or at school, and more bits of wisdom got added along the way.

In 1976, having completed my undergraduate education, I landed my first full-time civilian job working as a hospital pharmacist at a large teaching hospital. Two years later, when I became evening supervisor, I shared a desk with the supervisor on the day shift. One of my first orders of business was to get a bulletin board and mount it over the desk. My quotes and bits of wisdom, carefully stored in that envelope, went back on the wall, and I continued to add others. I established criteria for those I would add. In order to make it to the board, the quote, phrase, or idea had to be something that spoke to me with great power. Something that was profoundly applicable to working successfully with others. The kinds of things that make you sit straight up in bed when you read them, or the kinds of things that send you scrambling for a pen and paper when you hear them or even think them in the middle of the night. Many were products of reflection on powerful leadership lessons from my personal experiences and others from what had become voracious reading about great leaders of the past as I completed my graduate education at night and also completed a postgraduate fellowship.

2

MAXIM

A desk is a dangerous place from which to view the world.

—John le Carré

In 1969, I was a twenty-three-year-old first lieutenant in the US Army. I was serving as the ammunition officer of a field artillery service battery in Vietnam. I was assigned to a remote outpost called Bu Dop in an area known as the "Dog's Head" on the Cambodian Border. Our world included a dirt airstrip for fixed-wing aircraft, a perimeter of concertina wire, daily mortar attacks, and the continuous threat of nighttime ground assaults. Our days were long and hard. We received ammunition, food, and other supplies via fixed-wing aircraft and loaded that into CH-47 Chinook helicopter slings for distribution to firing batteries along the Cambodian border. Our battalion base camp was about eighty kilometers away. We were cut off from the outside world, and we never saw our battalion commander because he stayed in the relative safety and comfort of our base camp, often at his desk. Most people don't think of a desk when they think of Vietnam, but they were there. When our battalion commander completed his tour, a change of command ceremony took place at our base camp, but my guys and I weren't even there. My new battalion commander assumed command, and I didn't even know his name. For us, it would make no difference. He would remain back at base camp, and we would be in the field. Or so we thought.

As a first lieutenant, I was the highest-ranking officer assigned to Bu Dop at the time. At that point, I was pretty full of myself, and

I was a "take charge" kind of guy. One day, I was standing inside a CH-47 Chinook helicopter giving instructions to the crew chief. It was hot, the rotors were turning, and the air was filled with noise and the interminable red dust that was Vietnam in the dry season. I had my back to the ramp of the aircraft, and as the crew chief and I were shouting at each other to be heard, someone behind me was trying to get my attention. I turned and shouted, "Can't you see I'm busy right now? If you'll wait at the back of the aircraft, I'll get to you in a minute!" He immediately turned and did as I had told him.

When I turned back to the crew chief, he had a funny look on his face. He shouted at me, "That was a lieutenant colonel!"

Well, I was surprised and embarrassed. I'd never seen an officer of that rank at Bu Dop, and I had just insulted a field grade officer. I turned on my heel, went to the rear of the aircraft, rendered a full salute, and said, "My apologies, sir, how can I help you?"

To my amazement, with a big smile, he stuck out his hand and said, "Hi, Lieutenant Hester, I'm Frank Cartright, your new battalion commander. I've heard a lot about the work you guys are doing out here, and I wanted to come out and say hello… and I brought you some ice water." For the second time in a matter of seconds, I was surprised. Given my mistake, I had expected to be dressed down. Instead, I was greeted with a smile and a handshake. A man who would have been behaving normally had he stayed in the relative safety of our base camp had come to a dangerous outpost to introduce himself and to bring us ice water. That wasn't the end of it. He stayed with us overnight. He slept on a picnic table in our makeshift chow bunker, and he talked to us. He told us about himself. He asked us questions about our families. He wanted to know what we needed to do our job better. He described a safer bunker design he wanted us to build with materials he would send us, and he told us about the big picture in the tactical area around us. We asked him dozens of questions, and he answered them honestly. He told us that he wanted us to work hard, advance the mission, and stay safe. He said that getting the job done and getting us all home safely to our families were his two highest priorities. By the time he left in the morning, he had transformed our thinking about what we were doing, we had renewed purpose, and we felt connected to the big picture. We also knew that we had a battalion commander who knew us and cared about us. There wasn't anything we wouldn't do for him. In fact, Frank Cartright became one of the greatest influences in my leadership development. Frank Cartright didn't stop with us. He paid the same kind of visit to each of the several locations where members of our battalion were assigned, and when he finished, he did it again, and again. In addition to keeping us informed, he asked us for advice. He even asked us how he could be a better battalion commander.

Prior to his arrival, our artillery battalion had been a pretty average unit achieving pretty average results. Through his leadership, we became the highest-performing battalion in our artillery group. We were given the toughest assignments, and we carried them out to perfection. We were proud of our work, proud of ourselves, and proud to be led by Frank Cartright.

Frank Cartright had a desk at our base camp, but it was rarely used. He turned over responsibility for the things that needed to be done there to others. He was a frontline leader. He was always where the most important work was being done, and he was always with the frontline soldiers. He knew them, they knew him, and there wasn't anything they wouldn't do for him. Vietnam was a confusing war. Before Frank Cartright arrived, many of us were very uncertain about what we were doing and why we were there. After his arrival, we were doing it all for Frank Cartright, and that was all we needed to know. If it was good enough for the "old man," it was good enough for us. We knew him and we trusted him.

That environment was a crucible of learning for me. Every workweek was seven twenty-four-hour days, and the stakes were always high. Every month I was there, I acquired a year's worth of leadership learning and experience. Frank Cartright was a huge part of that. When my Vietnam tour was up, I extended it just to stay with him longer.

I carried this "frontline" lesson with me through the balance of my career. In every role I filled, I avoided my desk for large parts of the day. I built this away time into my calendar. Those who helped with my calendar knew my walk-and-talk time was important to me, and they worked hard to protect it. I walked, I talked, and I listened. Staff members came to know me, and I knew them. Through this critical activity, I acquired a genuine sense of their world. I understood the human condition among my work teams. Several times a week, they were presented with the opportunity to celebrate with me, share bad news with me, and give me advice when I needed it. Members of the staff came to know and feel the commitment I had for our mission and the passion I had for our vision. They knew that I was intensely interested in their world, and they knew that, along with the positives, I expected them to point out our challenges and shortcomings. Their managers and supervisors came to know that too. As a result, they were always hard at work looking for challenges and shortcomings themselves. Together, we did a good job of listening to, learning from, and enfranchising our frontline staff. It made all the difference.

I didn't limit this activity to frontline staff. When I met one-on-one with those who reported to me, I always went to their space instead of having them come to mine. This allowed me the opportunity to "be in their world," see their work environment firsthand, and talk with them about our work together on their turf. I learned so much more about them on their turf, and they had instant access to things we might talk about. Another huge advantage to this tactic is that it provided me with even more walk-and-talk time. I could pop my head in other offices along the route, greet and chat briefly with others in the corridor, or even go a little out of my way to thank or congratulate someone for good work, wish them a happy birthday, or just say hello. Doing this five or six times a week, times fifty or so weeks a year, is a lot of ground covered and a lot of interaction I would not have had otherwise. Not doing it would have represented a huge opportunity cost. It was a priceless activity.

In 1995, I had the privilege of stepping into a CEO role at a troubled community hospital. The medical staff and administration were at war, the physical plant was outdated, staff morale was low, the hospital's reputation in the community had suffered, it had done poorly on a regulatory accreditation visit, it was in serious financial trouble, and community leaders believed the hospital was nearing closure. While my confidence had grown substantially over the years, I was still very anxious. I was stepping in to lead an organization that was failing, and the risks to the served community were high. I went right to the playbook on my bulletin board. Along with extraordinary support from the health system and the application of sound business and organizational fundamentals, I engaged in the Frank Cartright method of leading. I made sure I had some interaction with almost everyone, on every shift, every day. I extended my presence to doctors' offices and into the community. I sought advice, asked for help, and became the organizations biggest cheerleader. I celebrated success where I found it, pointed out the positives, made peace where needed, and described a future state in which we would become the best rural hospital in America. After a few months, things began to turn around; and just a few years later, the same hospital became a premier provider among this nation's community hospitals. Today, the aging facility has been replaced by a brand-new, state-of-the-art hospital; it is in sound financial condition; it has been singled out by accreditation agencies as an example for other hospitals to follow; and staff and medical staff morale is very high. While the importance of the application of sound business and organizational fundamentals is undeniable in this story, the dramatic changes that fueled this wonderful turn-around story all came from the front line and from frontline leaders. They came from people who grew together and rallied around the changes needed to make all of this happen. That took help from everyone, connections, understanding, and communication at every level of the organization and into the community. My role was to serve as the agent and purveyor of the critical information and enthusiasm for the mission and vision that took. I could never, never, have done it from my desk or by myself.

Over the course of my career, I have observed that failure in leadership is often the result of being out of touch with reality. Many in leadership positions become mesmerized by the comfort of their office space and their desk. They view telephones, e-mail, and other forms of electronic and written communication to be all that is needed to assess their environment and lead their teams. Leaders who are the most successful don't fall victim to this dangerous trap. They are in touch with reality because they experience it firsthand, and I don't mean a twice-a-year event complete with a carefully staged photo for the employee newsletter. I mean getting out of the office and onto the field of play every day, because *a desk is a dangerous place from which to view the world!*

3

MAXIM

Eat in the cafeteria.

In almost all of my professional assignments, there has been a lunchroom, a cafeteria, or some sort of central gathering place for the midshift meal. For most of the world, that's lunch. Gathering for meals and breaking bread together is a tradition as old as man himself. There is something about the activity that generates comfort and goodwill among people. Walls come down, defenses are relaxed, and strong human bonds often form across the table; and you learn a lot about someone when you share a meal together.

When I was at the US Army Air Defense Board, it was during the days of mainframe computing. When my team had data to run, we had to get in the queue. We had to take our stack of punched IBM cards to the data center and then wait. It wasn't unusual to wait three or four days for our reports to be generated, and sometimes we had to reschedule the next trial flight of our target systems as a result. One day in the cafeteria, I shared a table with a Department of the Army Civilian I had not met before. We exchanged all of the appropriate politeness, and then I learned that he was in charge of the data center. I didn't bring up my challenge that day, but after eating with him two or three more times, I did. I simply asked. "Bob, I think you can give me some advice. Sometimes, we get held up on our project waiting for data…"

I didn't even get to finish my question. He said, "That shouldn't happen. Instead of dropping it off, just bring it to me." I did, and the turnaround time on our reports was cut in half. That could not have happened if I had not fallen into a relationship with Bob in the cafeteria. I made it my business there and in every organization I've been part of to eat in the cafeteria. I didn't eat with the same people every day either. I found new people to get to know, listen to, and learn from. Often I sat with complete strangers, but we didn't stay strangers after that. Honestly, in addition to helping me with my work, this was one of the most personally rewarding, educational, and satisfying things I did in my leadership journey. My friend Jim is the best example of that. Jim managed the end of the waste stream in our health system's largest hospital. His job was dirty, hot in the summertime, cold in the winter, and it could even be dangerous because of the potential exposure to infectious medical waste. Jim was a professional. He worked hard and supported the mission and vision of the health system. He got it, and Jim never had a bad day. In fact, Jim was always upbeat and happy. In spite of his working environment, which most people would be miserable in, Jim was genuinely glad to be part of the team contributing to our collective work. Every time I broke bread with Jim, I came away from the experience personally enriched and determined to be more like him. He was one of the complete strangers I sat down with in the cafeteria. Had I not done that, I would never have known him, and I would not have benefited from his inspiration. This was my practice throughout my career. When I moved to the executive suite, I continued the practice. It was not only still important, it actually became more important. Maybe I couldn't do it every day, but my goal was three days a week. Do the math. Three days a week times fifty or so weeks a year is one hundred fifty people or more reached and connected with every year that you might not even know otherwise. Over thirty-five years in the same health system, the number is staggering. It was better than any PhD I could have earned. I acquired priceless knowledge about the organization, I gained immeasurable influence, I made many wonderful friends, and my personal enrichment cannot be measured.

4

MAXIM

Don't accept unacceptable behavior.

In 1980, I was a department supervisor in our health system's flagship hospital. A new department director had been hired, and he was a different kind of leader from what I had ever experienced. He was new to the organization and held in very high regard by higher management, but he was cocky, arrogant, condescending, and he made it clear to all of us that we had a lot to learn from him.

During the first several months of his tenure, things got very hard at work. Morale declined, performance suffered, and I found myself, as supervisor, trying to motivate a team that was so unhappy with the boss that they couldn't focus on improving anything. To make matters worse, the new department director hired a clinical leader who was marginally competent and had poor people skills.

One of the department director's frequent behaviors was to have several of us come to his office to meet, close his door, and then smoke his pipe while we talked. By the time the meeting was over, the air would be blue, we would all be green around the gills, and one of my colleagues would become physically ill.

As things in the department continued to deteriorate, a few people left. I considered leaving and was interviewed for and offered another job; but in the end, I stayed, mostly because I felt an obligation to the good people I would leave behind, and in an odd way, I felt a need to protect them from the bad boss I was pretty sure the organization would eventually jettison. I also loved the health system and its mission. I couldn't bear the thought of this guy changing the trajectory of my career. I resolved to hunker down and protect our mission as well as the good people working hard to fulfill it to the best of my ability.

In addition to his other detractors, the department director was given to fits of anger that included use of objectionable language. During one of these events, he directed the worst kind of objectionable language at a female staff member in a very loud voice and slammed the door to his office with such force that it could all be heard throughout our large department. That event precipitated an anonymous report to the office of personnel, and that brought William to our department. William was an assistant vice president, and he was the department director's boss. William spent a couple of weeks quietly learning about the department, and he spent a lot of time going over reports and budgets with the department director. The department director got quiet during this period. He stayed in his office a lot and only said of William's time with him that he was familiarizing himself with the department's work.

Then, on a Monday morning, William held a brief meeting with everyone in the department to let us know that each of us would be scheduled for a one-on-one meeting with a staff member in personnel to talk about our work together. William told us that none of us had done anything wrong and that his intent was to help all of us create a positive work environment. He added a personal request that each of us answer questions we would be asked honestly, and he assured us that there would be no retribution from anyone. Those meetings took place; the questions the personnel representative asked centered around the department manager's behavior, and by the end of the next week, in a second brief meeting, William announced that the department manager was moving to a new role in the organization, effective immediately, and that the assistant director would assume interim leadership of the department during a search for the director's replacement.

There are two parts to the end of this story. The first part is that the new role for that department director was temporary, and he left the organization in short order. William wasn't willing to accept unacceptable behavior, and he made sure the organization did the right thing. The second part of the end of the story is that the department's assistant director ultimately became the new department director. He was competent in his role and, in every way, a gentleman. Morale soared, and over time, the department became one of the leading performers in the entire organization.

The most powerful lesson in this story is William. He wasn't willing to accept unacceptable behavior, and the difference that made for the department as well as the work of the organization was huge. A department that had become a below-average performer became one of the organization's best performers.

Over the course of my career, I have seen this same kind of story play out over and over. Bad actors demotivate others, poison the culture, and do untold damage to the organization's ability to perform. This is always a difficult circumstance, and especially so when the individual in question is technically competent, has extraordinary skills, or brings high value to the organization in other ways.

Years later, when I was assigned to one of our system's hospitals as president and CEO, a long-tenured physician, in a fit of temper, pulled a nurse's hair to demonstrate his anger over her execution of a treatment plan. As I investigated, I learned that similar things had also happened with the same physician before my arrival, and the Medical Staff Executive Committee had counseled him about his behavior. When I met with him to discuss the event, I informed him that pursuant to medical staff bylaws the Medical Executive Committee would investigate the incident. He told me that he would not meet with them but would resign first. I told him I would pick up his formal resignation letter from his office at the end of the day, and we lost a technically competent physician in a small community that couldn't afford to lose a doctor. Still, it was clearly the right thing to do. I thought about a lot of things as I did that, and one of them was William. The end of that story is that when the physician's departure from the medical staff became public knowledge, morale in the organization skyrocketed. With tears in her eyes, our director of nursing told me that no one in leadership had ever stood up for her staff like that before. Thanks for the lesson, William!

This lesson plays out on the corporate and organizational stage somewhere every day. Past revelations relating to tragic occurrences in and around more than one world-class athletic program are just one case in point. There, unacceptable behavior, even criminal behavior, was overlooked. The ultimate cost of that poor judgment has resulted in untold hurt to others and irreparable damage to the reputation of those organizations. It's just never, never, okay to accept unacceptable behavior.

5

MAXIM

When you communicate well, you succeed.
When you fail to communicate, you fail.

—Unknown

In leadership roles, if you communicate the right things well, you succeed. If you don't, you fail. But what do you communicate? And how do you do it?

Karl Weick, a Rensis Likert college professor of organizational behavior and psychology at the University of Michigan, teaches that work groups in challenging circumstances naturally attempt to rise to the occasion. He points out that people, by nature, are energized by challenge; and he says that even when the challenge rises to extraordinary levels, people will try very hard to rally to the cause, remain effective, and overcome the challenge, no matter how big. He says that extraordinary challenge improves morale among the group because they are so proud of their collective ability to take on the challenge and beat the odds.

But it's no surprise that Dr. Weick also says there are limits. When the challenge becomes too great, the organization breaks down and fails. The point on the challenge curve at which this occurs is a function of leadership. A well-led group will continue to be effective high into the challenge curve, but a marginally led group will break down lower on the challenge curve. It's all about leadership, and most of it boils down to communication.

In 1982, I had the privilege of participating in a fellowship at the University of Pennsylvania's Leonard Davis Institute, the post-graduate component of the Wharton School of Business. One of my professors, Dr. Michael Useem, expanded on Dr. Weick's work by making comparisons between groups who had broken down and failed under such circumstances and others who had, against incredible odds against them, succeeded. As we looked carefully at these cases, we surmised that if we could identify real-world groups (people doing anything together) that had been successful in spite of extraordinary challenge, then study the behaviors and attributes of their leaders, we would take away valuable lessons (*The Leadership Moment: Nine True Stories of Triumph and Disaster and Their Lessons For Us All* by Michael Useem, Three Rivers Press, New York). The study was compelling. For me, the exposure I had to these concepts in Dr. Useem's class and work propelled me on a journey of voracious reading, observing, and learning about leaders of the past and of the present that extended well beyond those studied during the fellowship. I focused my attention on real-life events that included stunning success as well as failure. I wanted to learn from real-life leaders in both instances. The good and the bad. I wanted to incorporate the behaviors of the good leaders into my leadership style and, of course, avoid the behaviors of the bad leaders. The leaders I studied included famous military leaders, well-known corporate CEOs, government leaders, explorers, civil rights activists, and astronauts.

As I engaged in this study, I found six common behaviors among leaders who were successful. I also learned that many, and sometimes all, of the same behaviors simply weren't practiced by those who failed.

Great "real world" leaders in history have consistently done the following:

Communicated a mission. They articulated it clearly and concisely. It was compelling, simply stated, and easy to understand. They weaved it into all of their communication with the people around them, over and over and over. Everyone came to see that mission as the only reason for the group's existence, and they repeated it to each other. Col. Joshua Lawrence Chamberlain, who led the Twentieth Maine Regiment at the Battle of Gettysburg, said over and over to anyone who would listen, "We are an army out to set other men free." Simply stated, easy to understand, and compelling.

Communicated a vision. They consistently and clearly described a desired future state. One that did not exist at the time, but one that was worth achieving. They repeated it over and over. Those around them adopted the vision as their own personal crusade. Colonel Chamberlain said, "America should be free ground, all of it. Not divided by a line between slave states and free. All the way, from here to the Pacific Ocean."

Again, it was simply stated, easy to understand, and compelling. The men of the Twentieth Maine came to see it as their personal crusade. One they would lay their lives down for without hesitation or question.

Communicated a few core values. These were simple but lofty ideals that formed the underpinning of all that the leaders believed. These they communicated through their words, and also through their behaviors and actions, over and over again. Colonel Chamberlain said, "No man has to bow. No man born to royalty. Here we judge you by what you do, not by who your father was. Here you can be something. Here is the place to build a home… We all have value… We're fighting for each other."

He lived these values out in every interaction with his men.

Communicated the context. Great leaders continually described external conditions and events around the organization and its work that was of significant impact and influence and offered support for, or challenges to, achieving the mission and vision of the organiza-tion. At a critical moment before the Battle of Gettysburg, speaking to a group of troublemakers who had just been assigned to his unit, Chamberlain said, "The whole reb army is up the road a ways wait-ing for us. We could surely use you fellows. We're now well below half strength. This regiment was formed last summer in Maine. There were a thousand of us then. There are less than three hundred of us now. I think, if we lose this fight, we lose the war." And then an appeal for them to pick up their arms and join the fight, but not before they had a full understanding of the context. Almost all of them did as he asked, and they contributed heavily to the successful outcome of the battle that followed.

Possessed and communicated, through words, behaviors, and actions, passion for the work of the group and for the group itself. Colonel Chamberlain was a man who revealed passion in all that he said and did. His focus on mission, vision, and values was continuous. To be in his presence was to be immersed in it all.

Possessed and communicated, through words and actions, empathy. In other words, they had a genuine appreciation for the human condition, and that played out in their everyday interactions with others. Colonel Chamberlain knew his men. He formed a relationship with each one. While he was their colonel, he was never hesitant to reveal his humanity, listen to advice, and learn from those he led. Even though he was an officer, he wore the cap traditionally worn by the enlisted men, and he often walked with the men instead of riding his horse.

Colonel Chamberlain and the Twentieth Maine Regiment prevailed at Gettysburg in spite of nearly impossible odds, leading a bayonet charge when all of the 20th Maine's ammunition was depleted. Chamberlain himself received the Congressional Medal of Honor for what he and the 20th Maine did there. Many civil war historians credit Chamberlain with the Union victory at Gettysburg, which turned the tide of the war in the Union's favor at a critical time.

Chamberlain communicated the right things in the right way. Not just once. He understood that he needed to be engaged in continual communication with his men about mission, vision, values, and context. He did that with the passion he felt, and he did it with a deep sensitivity to the human condition of the Civil War soldier.

Real-world examples of these same behaviors among well-known successful leaders of the past abound in history. If you have a hero among these past leaders, use this yardstick to measure his or her behavior among those they led. Almost, without exception, you'll find that they engaged in these behaviors. These are just six things that make all the difference when done well. Not doing them almost guarantees failure.

- Overcommunicate a mission.
- Overcommunicate a vision
- Overcommunicate a few core values.
- Overcommunicate the context.
- Possess and overcommunicate passion.
- Possess and overcommunicate empathy.

6

MAXIM

Every problem is an opportunity in disguise.

—John Adams

In 1985, I had been serving our health system's teaching hospital as the administrative director of pharmacy for a little over five years. I loved my work, but we had built a very strong department that functioned well even when I wasn't there. I had also completed my graduate education, and I was anxious to do and learn more. I reported to an assistant vice president named Dave, and during our one-on-one business meetings, I always offered to take on project work outside of my department. Because things were going well in the pharmacy, I had capacity, and I knew there were a lot of needs throughout the health system. One of the things I told Dave was that I was willing to take on anything, including headaches no one else wanted.

At that time, housekeeping services were provided to our medical center by a third-party contractor. Simply put, it wasn't working, and repeated attempts to improve the service had failed. It was a source of great frustration to leadership because cleanliness in the hospital business is critical. Not only because it's important to look your best but because an unclean hospital can be a dangerous place for patients and staff. Because many people feel that housekeeping isn't the most glamorous side of the health-care business, none of the junior administrators were standing in line to take on the challenge.

One morning after arriving at work, I got a telephone call from Dave. He asked if I would be willing to meet with the medical center's CEO to discuss a possible project. Dave described it as a project that involved evaluating our options relative to housekeeping. I jumped at the chance and met with the CEO later that morning, and two weeks later, having temporarily assigned responsibility for the operations of the Pharmacy Department to a very capable assistant director, I immersed myself in the world of housekeeping as an "internal consultant."

It's important to understand a few things here. First, I was a pharmacist. At that time, it took five years to earn a pharmacy degree. I had to pass a state licensing exam, and I had also completed a clinical clerkship as a postgraduate. I had spent years preparing myself to practice pharmacy in the hospital setting, and I was stepping away from all of that to serve as a full-time internal consultant in matters regarding housekeeping. My mother was not impressed. At the same time, I had a very strong attraction to broader leadership in the health-care setting, and my interests had expanded to everything that should be done to create a perfect environment within which talented health-care professionals could provide great care to members of my community. So this problem, this job that was undesirable to some, was clearly an opportunity for personal growth and self-mastery. Finally, the fact that the president & CEO of the teaching hospital had taken a personal interest in this project, and had extended power and authority to me to complete my work, was a huge factor. While I did not know him well at that time, all of my exposure to him in the past had been very positive. I trusted him. I believed that if I took good care of the organization, the organization would, in some way, take reasonable care of me, and that was enough.

Over the next several weeks, I engaged in all of the behaviors of a good consultant. I made my entry, developed relationships with the leadership team as well as the housekeepers, collected data, analyzed it, provided feedback to the housekeeping leadership, shared summary reports with the president and CEO, developed alternative short- and long-term solutions, shared those with the CEO, and at the end of the fourth week, included my recommendation as to which solution we should implement.

My recommendation to the president and CEO was that we discontinue our contract with the third-party provider and bring the service in-house. The formal agreement we had with the third-party provider was flawed, their leadership team had proven itself unable to make necessary changes, and the regional manager had been unable to help.

Because implementation of the recommendation meant that we would lose all of the contractor's leadership team, all of their policies and procedures, and all of their equipment and cleaning supplies, it would be a huge undertaking and the time table would be critical. Hospitals never close, and they never take a day off. We'd have to hit the ground running, with our own infrastructure in place, at midnight of the last contract day. I had included a complete assessment of the hospital-employed hourly staff in the department during my initial work, and I was confident we could be successful with the addition of some outside expertise and talent, but it was the CEO's decision to make.

It was during a hastily scheduled meeting in follow-up to my proposal that the president and CEO told me the president of the third-party provider had been his college roommate. But he accepted my recommendation with the understanding that I would personally lead the initiative to bring the service in-house and that he would be the one to call his former college roommate to break the bad news. Of course, I agreed.

The next several weeks and few months were filled with intensity. The two-hundred-plus staff members in the Housekeeping Department had been pretty unhappy working for the third-party contractor, and they were thrilled to have some influence in their professional destiny. Most of them wanted to be proud of their work, and they weren't. I quickly included them in decision-making, divided them up into formal teams, and from the best and most experienced, appointed formal team leaders. Because we had to acquire all new equipment and supplies, I formed a task force of about fifteen experienced individuals to oversee that part of the process, and I did the same thing for the development of policies and procedures.

I asked a couple of superstars from other departments in the health system to consider coming on board to serve in supervisory roles, and they did. Finally, I approached a major supplier of health-care environmental services equipment and supplies and offered to negotiate an exclusive short- and long-term purchase agreement with them if they would give us unlimited access to their expertise during the transition. We were able to negotiate a fair agreement, and they quickly provided outside expertise to both internal task forces.

The end of this story is one of great success. The staff felt liberated and empowered and accepted full ownership for their department and its role in the organization. The exclusive supplier came through with policy and procedure templates and all of the equipment and supplies we needed. On the last day of the contract, the contractor's trucks backed up to the loading dock and hauled everything away. Every piece of equipment, all of the chemicals, every mop, every broom, all the rags, and the contractor's leadership team left with them. We were on our own. The new supplier's trucks, waiting nearby, backed up to the loading dock and replaced them all with brand-new stuff our team had purchased. By sunup, it was all accounted for, mostly operational, and a small army of tired but enthusiastic housekeepers spread out across the campus to do their work. There were high fives all around.

Over the next several months, things got better and better. The hospital was clean again. Job satisfaction among housekeepers improved dramatically, and the serious operational and personnel problems that had plagued the department diminished.

For me, this adventure was an incredible learning and growth process. It afforded me the opportunity to test the theories of leadership I had learned in the first years of my journey, and it affirmed my faith in the fact that almost everyone wants to perform well. I was permitted the opportunity to hire a permanent full-time director of housekeeping to replace me, and I gratefully and humbly accepted a new job offer as assistant vice president of administrative services for the medical center.

7

MAXIM

Before you can manage others, you must first manage yourself.
—Steven Covey

In 1985, at the age of thirty-nine, I was a mid-level leader in our health system's teaching hospital. As I learned from and observed the senior leaders around me, Frank stood out as being the most organized and on top of everything. He always displayed confidence and extraordinary competence. When I met with him in his office, I noticed that his desk had nothing on it: just a phone, a writing pad, and a pen. That's it. This was in stark contrast to my desk which always had several piles on it along with a series of baskets: an "in" basket, a "hold" basket, an "out" basket, and even a "maybe never" basket.

Frank was one of the most senior leaders in the organization. I knew that he had more responsibility than I did, that he interacted with more people than I did, and that a lot more work went through his office than went through mine. Naturally I wondered how he could have a clean desk, be so in control, and never appear stressed, so I asked Frank to tell me his secret.

His response was simple: "I have a suspense file, and I use my calendar to keep track of and plan my work and to manage deadlines." I had never heard of a suspense file, so I asked Frank if, at another time, he could take a few minutes and show me how his suspense file/calendar method worked. He agreed. We set up a meeting and here is what Frank showed me:

1. Frank's suspense file was one drawer in a lateral file with thirty-one hanging files in it. Each of the thirty-one files corresponded to a date on the calendar. They were simply numbered one through thirty-one.

2. Each of the folders had papers in them that related directly to the work or project on which Frank needed to work on the date corresponding to the number of the hanging file they were in.

3. If a document or documents were designated for that numerical date two or more months away, they were clipped together and had the month and date notated on the front so that they wouldn't be confused with the first occurrence of that date.

4. His calendar also had notations about the work or project in the files, which served as a reminder to him to do the work on that day, and also to reserve the needed time for actually doing the work.

5. As I looked at Frank's calendar, I could see that it was filled not only with meetings and events; it included lots of notations about projects and desk work he had to do which filled the time slots required to complete the work.

6. At the end of each work day, Frank would quickly review his calendar for the coming day to remind himself what work he would be doing the following day. In the morning, he would retrieve the needed documents from the suspense file.

7. Finally, as new work requirements came to him, Frank would consider the deadline requirements, identify the date on his calendar when he would do that work, reserve the time to do the work, and then place the documents in the corresponding day's suspense file.

Frank explained to me that his method was dynamic. He said that he sometimes had to make adjustments to his calendar that required adjustments to his project calendar. When that happened, he always made the calendar adjustments, moved the documents in his file and, if necessary, negotiated a new deadline with others who depended on his completed work.

Well, I was hooked. I spent the next several weeks learning to make Frank's method work for me. It took persistence and discipline because I had a strong tendency to fall back into my old style of managing myself. After about three weeks, I finally had it working well. It changed how I thought about work, improved the quality of my work, and increased my confidence on the job. Here's what was different.

Before I adopted Frank's method, desk and project work always took a back seat to the tyranny of the moment. All of the unexpected things that came up every day often prevented me from getting that work done, so I had to work very late in the day or come in on weekends to complete it.

After I implemented Frank's method, that still happened sometimes, but I found over time that I was able to control my time a lot better. As an example, if an unexpected requirement got in the way of completing desk work on a previously planned day, and if I could still meet the deadline by sliding the previously planned work ahead a day or two, I could move it in the suspense file and on my calendar. This practice gave me a lot of peace of mind because I knew I would not lose track of it, and the time to do the work was reserved on my calendar. Conversely, if I ever found unexpected time on my hands due to a cancellation, I could reach forward on my project calendar, retrieve the documents, and get work done ahead of plan.

Before I implemented Frank's method, I had a lot of work-related anxiety. I was constantly thinking about, and worrying about, deadlines and various pieces of work so that I didn't forget something or fall so far behind that I simply did not have the time to meet my work requirements. This included my time at home. Instead of being focused on my family, I was often mulling over and thinking about work.

After I implemented Frank's method, the work-related anxiety diminished significantly. At any given moment I knew without doubt that every piece of desk or project work was accounted for, carefully recorded on my calendar with time reserved to do the work, and the corresponding documents were close at hand when the time came to do it, but they weren't cluttering my desk. For me, the new peace of mind was huge. I felt in control.

Before I implemented Frank's method, I often found myself lacking confidence that I could be successful in the high pressure environment in which I was working. I didn't know if I could keep track of and manage the sheer volume and complexity of the work.

After I implemented Frank's method, my confidence grew dramatically. I found that I could take on more work, that I was getting it done in less time, that my level of work-place anxiety had diminished, and that I felt in control.

Perhaps most important of all, before I implemented Franks method, I spent way too much of my time and energy on juggling my time and project work and not nearly enough time actually leading those around me. By leading, I mean keeping in touch with them, listening to and learning from them, encouraging them, and helping them be successful in their own roles.

After implementing Frank's method, with renewed confidence and more time, I was able to focus a lot more of my time leading. I was more relaxed, felt more in control, and could truly focus on listening to, learning from, and helping members of my team.

I incorporated Frank's method into my professional life from then on and I never looked back. It became a habit. All of the baskets disappeared from my desk, and at the end of the day, my desk top was always clear. I began to look and act more like Frank. Most important though is that I became as effective as Frank. By learning how to manage myself better, I freed up a lot of time and energy for leading. I am grateful for the time Frank spent describing his suspense file/calendar method and for serving as a great role model for me.

8

MAXIM

The next great leader may not be obvious.

While I was serving as director of pharmacy for our health system's teaching hospital, I met Jeff. Jeff was a pharmacy technician. He was a good one. He knew his stuff, and he was accurate, dependable, and he finished his work on time.

Some of the other pharmacy technicians in the department were different. They were sometimes late to work, a few often missed work, some struggled with accuracy, and some with getting their work finished on time. They were the ones that got most of my attention while Jeff and the others, more like him, got less of my attention. In many ways I was guilty of taking the good ones for granted. They became almost transparent to me, and because at that time, there was no career ladder for pharmacy technicians, I never thought of Jeff as a potential leader. While he was a solid pharmacy technician performing his job very well, I never observed anything in his behavior indicating a potential to lead. He was outgoing enough, and pleasant, but he just didn't stand out. A lot of days he kept his nose in his work and was pretty quiet.

One of the pharmacists in our department lived on a small horse farm and it was his habit to hold a big party at his place each year for everyone on staff. There were about twenty-four of us in the department at that time, so about thirty-five or forty people would show up at the outing. It was a big deal and a lot of fun. It always included a big feed, horse back riding, and horse shoes.

One year we were told on the invitation that there was to be a scavenger hunt and we all showed up at the party, not knowing exactly how the scavenger hunt would unfold. After the usual activities, it was time for the scavenger hunt, and who should jump up on a tabletop to describe the event but Jeff.

Jeff totally took charge. He described the hunt, shared the list of things we would be looking for, quickly divided us up into teams, shared rules about boundaries, safety, and so forth, then sent us on our way. During the hunt, he kept us informed about time remaining via a huge megaphone, reassembled us at the end of the event, and awarded prizes. He did all of this with great humor. It was a blast. Everyone thoroughly enjoyed it, and Jeff pulled it all off without a hitch, as if he had done it dozens of times before.

Later, I asked the host of the party about the event, and I learned that he had asked Jeff to do it. Jeff had never done anything like that before but told the host he would give it a try. Wow. I was amazed, and I privately felt a little foolish. Oh sure, a scavenger hunt is just a game, but I saw, through this event, abilities in Jeff that I had never seen or even suspected before. His ability to develop a plan, communicate with others about it, execute the plan with them, and do it all with near perfection, while having a lot of fun in the process, demonstrated skills that were transferable to the workplace. I never forgot it, and I never saw Jeff in the same way again.

Winding the calendar forward a few months, I was given the opportunity to take on a hospital wide problem-solving assignment outside of my department. Among other things, due to the termination of an outsourced contract, it included the need to quickly replace the manager of the hospital's laundry department. We did not have time to engage in a long search for a replacement, and no one in the department was interested in filling the role, not even on a temporary basis. I had to get someone to lead the department right away.

As I considered all of my options, I was reminded of Jeff. I knew he was dependable and that he had good communication and organizational skills. I knew that he learned quickly, was likable, and that he was willing to work hard. I decided to see if Jeff would agree to filling the role on a temporary basis until we could find a permanent replacement.

When I met with Jeff, he was surprised but enthusiastic about the opportunity. He told me he would give it his best shot. That was good enough for me.

Because Jeff had no experience in a hospital laundry department, I arranged, through our chemicals supplier, to send Jeff to their headquarters city where he could do a two-week crash course in hospital laundry operations that included working inside of one of their large hospital laundry customer's facility.

Jeff came back from that experience excited and ready for the job. He started immediately, connected with the staff, quickly took care of some long-standing equipment problems, and addressed several nagging staff complaints too. He didn't try to hide the fact that he was new. He actively sought out advice from his staff and shared some of the things he had learned during his crash course. He took the work very seriously, but he made life fun again in a department that just hadn't been fun for a long time. Things got better quickly, and over a few months, everything improved dramatically. Internal customer satisfaction improved, staff morale skyrocketed, and operating costs went down.

Jeff and I had never discussed what would happen at the end of his temporary assignment. We had generally agreed that it might be three or four months, so as time passed, and we needed to search for a permanent replacement, I asked Jeff for his advice. After a thoughtful pause, he asked, "Do you think I would be considered if I applied?"

While I needed to get approval from others, it didn't take long. The improvements in the service had been significant and very welcome. The organization was grateful to Jeff, and our culture was very supportive of identifying and growing talent from within.

Jeff got the job permanently, and he did a wonderful job leading a critical department in the hospital. Over time, he and his team upgraded a lot of outdated equipment and implemented new procedures that enhanced safety and efficiency. Staff satisfaction soared to new heights.

For me, that serendipitous scavenger hunt of a few months before had opened my eyes to qualities in Jeff I should have seen before. *I was reminded how important it was for me, no matter how busy, to observe the people around me more deeply, and, as opportunities arose, to test them with more responsibility.*

Winding the clock forward a few years, I was given the opportunity to lead a community hospital that was newly acquired by our health system. It was a hospital that was in trouble. Administration and the medical staff were at war, the hospital was in financial trouble, staff morale was at an all-time low, and the hospital had performed poorly on an accreditation review.

One of the first things I had to do was restructure the leadership team. Among other changes in structure and reassignment of responsibilities, that exercise resulted in the elimination of a senior leader position that was problematic and unnecessary. The person who occupied the role left the organization and I needed a good, mid-level operations leader who could assume responsibility for multiple departments. I wanted to find someone from inside the organization, if possible, so I began my search.

I had already been working hard on getting to know all of the department heads and managers in the hospital. Some stood out, but there was one who really interested me. Her name was Pam. She was the supervisor of medical records and also responsible for a pool of medical transcriptionists.

Pam interested me because her department had a solid reputation in the hospital, she never got caught up in any of the drama going on around her, and she had given me some great advice regarding the medical staff when I came in the door. She had a better relationship with the medical staff than almost anyone else in the hospital. She was a peacemaker, and the doctors viewed her as an ally.

Pam's office was at the opposite end of the same long hallway my office occupied. I was at one end, she was at the other, and the elevator and the medical records department were right in the middle. While she was well respected within the organization, she kept a pretty low profile. Medical records was not on the beaten path to or from anywhere in the hospital. She often took lunch in her office, and while she did sit on a few important committees, she had no significant role outside of medical records.

Every doctor came to medical records several times a week to review and sign off on medical records. One of the first things I noticed is that many of them stopped in to chat with Pam while they were there. They sought her advice and counsel on matters relating to medical records, but also on other matters relating to the hospital. It was clear to me that they respected Pam and valued her department's critical contribution to the care of their hospitalized patients. They valued her advice about other things too.

So I broached the subject with Pam of considering a larger role with expanded responsibility. She said "no" in no uncertain terms. She said that administration just wasn't for her and she really liked what she was doing. She didn't even want to discuss it, so I left her alone for a while.

Over the course of the next several weeks, I asked Pam to take on a couple of small but important projects outside of her direct area of responsibility. While never discussed, those were tests for both of us. I got to see how she performed outside of her wheelhouse, and she got to experience working outside of her comfort zone. She did well and I thanked her.

I allowed some time to pass, then I asked Pam how she felt about the project work. She said that she enjoyed the change of pace and was happy that she had been able to contribute. I asked her if she would consider similar, and possibly even bigger, special projects in the future. She said that she would. I asked her if she had enough depth in her department to pick up some slack for her while she took on project work. She told me about Beth. Beth was her most capable and trusted medical records specialist, and she was already providing leadership and guidance to the staff alongside Pam.

So I asked her, "What do you fear the most about permanently accepting a greater role and more responsibility in the organization? You're more than capable of filling such a role, and the medical records department will be fine. In fact, it sounds like it would allow Beth to grow professionally too." Her response was slower in coming than when we had had the first conversation on the subject. She said that she was uncomfortable in the public eye and was afraid of how her promotion would be perceived by her peers.

I assured her that both of those things were common fears, but that they were very manageable, and that her anxiety about them was much bigger than either of them warranted. After a pause, she said, "I suppose."

I quickly put together a job description and formally offered Pam the position of "director of operations" the next day. I gave her the rest of the week and the weekend to decide. She took all of that time before accepting the job with some apprehension.

Over the next several years, Pam not only met but exceeded my expectations. Our hospital's operational and clinical performance improved dramatically, and we scored very well on accreditation surveys. Pam was instrumental in helping me restore a strong partnership between hospital administration and the medical staff. She ultimately became the director of operations and assistant administrator of the hospital, which was the role she held when she retired. In addition, during a time of transition at the health system level, Pam temporarily filled the role of corporate compliance officer for the entire health system. She handled that critically important and complex job very well and quickly earned the respect of system senior leadership.

Pam was unlikely to lead at the level she ultimately did because, at one time, she could not see herself in such roles. Just thinking about it made her uncomfortable. She had to be forced to see the possibilities, but once she did, she jumped in with both feet and set the standard for other leaders in the system.

Look deeply for leadership potential around you. Sometimes, it's right there under your nose.

In Jeff's case, I was blind to it until it was revealed to me in an accidental and serendipitous way. Jeff's leadership benefited the organization at a critical time and got a critical department squarely back on track.

In Pam's case, I saw the potential, but she was very reluctant to step out of her comfort zone. It took testing the waters and some gentle persuasion. Her leadership to the organization over the next fifteen years was extraordinary. In addition, Beth did an outstanding job leading the medical records department until she retired.

Look deeply for leadership potential among those around you. It's often not obvious.

9

MAXIM

It's not about you.

—Rick Warren

Immediately following completion of officer candidate school and the Air Defense Artillery Officer Basic Course, I was assigned to McGregor Range, New Mexico. I was twenty-two years old and a brand-new second lieutenant with no experience as a military officer. I was really lucky to get this particular assignment because I got to work for John. It was my job to be trained by and assist him. John was a first lieutenant, and he was the first army officer I was exposed to who taught me by example how to be a successful and extraordinarily effective leader in the military.

Formally, John's job was that of range control and safety officer, and it was a huge responsibility. At McGregor, we oversaw training and test firings of Nike Ajax, Nike Hercules, and Hawk antiaircraft missiles in a carefully controlled airspace directly over about 650,000 acres of New Mexico desert. The range was bordered by two state highways and a safe air corridor between McGregor and adjacent White Sands Missile Range, which was routinely used by commercial and civilian aircraft. For John, and for all of us that worked for him, precision and safety were paramount.

The stereotypical authoritarian style of leadership one might expect in the army didn't exist at range control. Nothing about John's behavior was about him, and his behavior was anything but authoritarian. Instead, John's focus was all about the mission, the people around him, and his relationship with each one. Before entering the army, he had been a teacher by profession, and it showed. He was patient, thorough, and kind; and while the importance of our work was made crystal clear to all of us, he made it fun. To a casual observer, unless John was sitting in the chair of the range control officer as he did during a shoot, it would have been hard to pick out who was in charge. He just wasn't a command-and-control kind of leader. Instead, he made sure those around him were properly trained and equipped to do their assigned job well, and then he attended to his.

Our small group of about a dozen individuals occupied the range control tower at McGregor. It sat up on a hill on the southern boundary of the range looking north. It was kind of out of the way with a winding drive that rose up off of the desert floor to a small parking lot. One of the things I noticed right away was that during range downtime, all kinds of people who did not work directly for John, but who were critical to the functioning of the range, frequently came up that drive to see him. They would grab a cup of coffee and then just sit and talk about various things going on at the range as well as sports, swap a story or two, and then be on their way. People like the range communication officer, the explosive ordnance disposal NCO, and others. Their visits were really unnecessary to the mission, or so it seemed, but I quickly learned that the fact that John had that kind of relationship with people all over the range was what made us so successful. They didn't have to come and see him, but they wanted to. He was well liked and well respected by everyone. John's demeanor with everyone, including his frequent visitors, made him the sort of man people wanted to be friends with. He was genuinely interested in each one of them. As he introduced each one of them to me, he included some well-deserved praise about their work and their contribution to the mission. During shoots, when the chips were down, no one questioned or challenged his direction. Not just because he was the sitting range control officer, but because they knew him, liked him, and respected him. That might have been different if he did not already have a strong relationship with each one of them.

An unfortunate part of the mission was that various weapon systems being tested sometimes started range fires in the dry New

Mexico desert. The responsibility for coordinating the extinguishing of the fire and providing navigational assistance to the firefighters fell on our doorstep. Often, the fires took a long time to isolate and extinguish, and dealing with them was almost always at the end of a long shoot day. That meant a lot of after-hours work. John could have gone home, leaving the rest of us to coordinate the effort, but he didn't. He stayed. Not because anything was required of him, but because he just wanted to be there to show his support for the rest of us as we did our jobs. It was never about him; it was about us and his support of us.

Over the course of my five years in the army, John was the first officer who taught me by example how to lead effectively; not by giving orders, but by quietly building relationships, building trust and credibility, and taking full advantage of the talent around him. There would be others like him to follow, and just like John, they would be the most effective. In contrast, I spent time with still others who were focused on themselves. Their own achievement, advancement, and self-promotion. They were authoritarian leaders, and it was clear to me that they had no real interest in the people around them. They achieved results too, but it wasn't the same. People did for them what they had to do to stay out of trouble. They often got the job done, but that was all. Their people often did not seek an extraordinary outcome, just the outcome that represented a job done by average measure. The different results I observed by the two leadership styles were so much that it made a lasting impact on my personal leadership development. Not just in the army, but forever. I wanted to be just like John and the others like him. *I learned not to value myself as much as I valued the people around me and the relationships I built with each one of them. I also learned that I simply could not achieve any real degree of success without the full support and passion of the people around me because they wanted all of us together to be wildly successful. It really wasn't about me. Not ever.*

10

MAXIM

Anger is a bad counselor.

—French proverb

At a point during my tenure as CEO of a small rural hospital, due to changes in reimbursement for ambulance care, and because it would be in the overall best interest of the served community, I notified the county that the hospital would not renew its contract to run the county's ambulance program at the end of the contract period.

Although we allowed several months' notice, it was an uncomfortable surprise to most county officials because the hospital had provided the service for so many years that there wasn't anyone serving as a county official who remembered a different arrangement, and they weren't even sure how to proceed.

I offered to provide guidance and put them in touch with willing providers of a restructured service, and they accepted my offer. After introducing them to the regional contenders to become the new contract provider, county officials developed a request for proposal that was circulated to the contenders.

Surprisingly, in addition to eventual proposals received from the three established providers of ambulance services in nearby communities, a small group of paramedics employed by the hospital submitted a proposal to form a new company and provide the service to the county themselves.

In a discussion with one of the county officials, I privately expressed the opinion that the small group of paramedics probably lacked the background, experience, and credentials to make such a venture successful. The county official chose to share my opinion at a public meeting. It was picked up by the press, and I was the target of a very unflattering editorial piece in the community newspaper.

I was angry at the county official for publicly sharing my opinion, I became angry at the small group of paramedics for what I felt at the time was nothing more than an unfortunate complication in the process, and I was especially angry at the local editorial writer who I felt unfairly characterized my motives.

While I had intended to refrain from public engagement in the matter, my anger caused me to fully engage, and I became a vocal public advocate for encouraging county officials to choose one of the established providers and not the small group of paramedics.

Over the course of several weeks, the question divided the community, and a large group of supporters, including a well-known community physician champion, stepped forward in support of the group of paramedics. In addition to their morale support, they raised money and committed to hiring a qualified individual to organize and run the service. The paramedics ultimately won the contract, and it all became a very unfortunate incident of winners and losers with the hospital and me on the losing end.

And it did not have to be that way. Had I not let my anger get the best of me and had I not gone on the offensive, the outcome might have been different, and at least the end result would not have been viewed by some as a "winners and losers" incident. It was my fault that it did. Because I let my anger drive my thinking and my actions, and I was also blind to the possibilities of providing additional support to the paramedics to help them to be successful. The reality is that the paramedics' plan worked. They were and are still successful. I was wrong, and it was because I allowed my anger to cloud my thinking and influence my response. *Never, never, submit to anger. Instead, defer action, cool off, and think it through.*

11

MAXIM

Every day is a second chance.

—Unknown

On May 1, 1970, the Field Artillery Service Battery I led participated in the invasion of Cambodia. While we did not cross the border into Cambodia, our mission was to coordinate the resupply of food, water, construction material, and ammunition to the firing batteries in our battalion that did. We convoyed the materials to a lift site near the border, prepared helicopter sling loads, and then hooked the material out to the firing batteries with CH-47 Chinook helicopters. This was a routine operation for us, but normally, we had the selected lift site all to ourselves. This time, the lift site we were using was being used by several other units doing the same thing. There were often several CH-47 helicopters orbiting the lift site, waiting for their turn to come in and pick up their loads. Visibility was poor due to blowing dust, the noise level was very high, and the strong prop wash of the dual-rotor CH-47s created challenges for all of us. The weather was also a factor, and wind gusts were challenging for the pilots of the CH-47s. Under normal circumstances, we might have called a weather hold, and it was also very unusual to engage in this work in such close proximity to others doing the same thing.

Some of the food and other supplies we were sending to the field were contained inside of large metal containers called Conexes. Basically, a Conex was a big steel box sealed with a door. Those we were using were about six feet by eight feet by eight feet. Once filled with supplies, the door was sealed, lifting straps were attached, and then we stood on top of the Conex holding the straps over our heads while the CH-47 eased in to hook the load. When the hook was within reach, the man standing on the Conex would slap the strap's "doughnut" into the hook and climb down, and the CH-47 would take the Conex away.

Late in the day, I was on top of one of these Conexes. As the CH-47 approached, the pilot was having a hard time controlling his position because of high winds. He came in so low that instead of standing on top of the Conex, I was forced into a low crouch and then was even forced to lie down on my back. I was face-to-face with the CH-47's crew chief looking down at me through the center hatch, and I could see the concern on his face turn to alarm as he frantically informed the pilot via his intercom radio that he was too low. Still, the CH-47 came lower and pinned me to the top of the Conex. I couldn't move, and I could feel my breath being forced out of me as more and more weight pressed down. I could no longer breathe, I began to feel myself losing consciousness, and in that instant, I knew I was going to die. Throughout my Vietnam experience, I had often been concerned about getting home, but I had never dreamed I'd be crushed by one of our own helicopters. And then there was a very brief release of pressure as the CH-47 rose up in the wind. I rolled as hard and fast as I could to one side and fell off of the conex. A split second later, the CH-47 bounced off of the Conex, denting the top of it. I was dazed and couldn't catch my breath for several minutes. The guys who had been on the other side of the Conex hadn't seen me roll off, and at first, they thought I had been crushed. I was sore for several days but escaped serious injury, and for the first time in my life, I was overwhelmed with just being alive. It was crystal clear to me that in that instant, I could have died, but through a miracle, I didn't. I knew that day, and have known every day since, that each new day is an extraordinary gift from God. It has been as if, in that instant, a switch was turned on inside of me. All that had happened before was only of minor importance. What became extraordinarily important from that moment on was using each new day to do good work and to make a meaningful difference in the lives of others.

And so it is for all things. Perhaps not quite so profoundly, but no matter what happened, or didn't happen yesterday, today is a second chance.

You've never lived until you've almost died.
(Guy de Maupassant)

12

MAXIM

Heads up. The "twelfth maxim" is a different kind of maxim. A timeless truth to be sure, but a practical model is also provided. Understanding the model requires focus. It's really important. The "twelfth maxim" is perfect for group discussion and shared learning among leadership study groups.

Successful human capital management is the driving
force behind sustained competitiveness.

We have all heard some variation of this during our professional journey, and almost none of us would deny that it's a fact. But how many of us have taken it so seriously that we developed and implemented specific tactics that intentionally leverage human capital management in the pursuit of excellence?

Previously, I described the turnaround of a troubled community hospital. While many things contributed to that, human capital management was a big part. The senior management team, each of us starting with ourselves, applied something we called the "willing and able" method of managing human capital. While significantly tailored to our specific need, our approach was partly based on some elements of Paul Hersey and Ken Blanchard's situational leadership theory as well as similar models we had all been exposed to in the past.

When we had applied our tool and completed an evaluation of ourselves, we pushed it down through the rest of the organization.

Here's the logic behind what we did and why we did it.

If you were hired to manage a major league baseball team, and the owner told you he or she expected you to win the pennant three years out of the next five (the length of your contract), you'd go right to work on human capital. For you, that would be job one, and you'd have to field a team of standout, willing, and able players to meet that expectation.

It's exactly the same in your company or work group. Most of us, metaphorically speaking, want to "win the pennant" at work. We want the performance of our company or work team to be the stuff of legends. That requires a lineup of standout, willing, and able team members. There simply isn't room for average, or below average, performance. If you settle for that, no pennant, and your performance will never become the stuff of legends.

Here's how the "willing and able" method works.

In the world at work, in order for an individual to be a true standout, they have to be willing to engage in certain behaviors and avoid other behaviors, and they have to be able to do certain things better than 90 percent of their peers close to 100 percent of the time.

They must be willing

- to respect and regard others' views;
- to share power, knowledge, and responsibilities;
- to take risks and learn new things;
- to give and to receive constructive feedback;
- to speak for self, i.e., "I want…, I feel…";
- to listen attentively and with empathy; and
- to challenge norms, disagree constructively, and in the end, commit to the ultimate decision.

They must be able

- to perform assigned responsibilities effectively and consistently;
- to remain focused on real and relevant issues;
- to demonstrate congruence between statements and practice;
- to solve problems effectively;
- to avoid and to resolve unhealthy conflict;
- to demonstrate creative and effective use of resources; and
- to demonstrate clear and predictable patterns of communication.

Using these measures to assess your team members can help to reduce subjectivity. While imperfect, it provides a kind of yardstick to see where you are with your work group when you walk in the door, or when you decide to get serious about human capital.

Each of the fourteen attributes above can be scored on a 1–10 scale for each member of the team. A 10 is reserved for individuals who may be the best you've ever seen regarding the attribute you are considering. A 1 is reserved for the worst you've ever seen. When all of the attributes for "willing" have been scored, you can plot an arithmetical average on the grid below (figure 1), and then do the same for the attributes for "able" ("willing" on the vertical axis and "able" on the horizontal axis). Now find the point on the grid where those two measures intersect, make a dot, and place the individual's initials next to it. This tells you where that individual falls relative to their unique "willing and able" profile.

Those who truly are the standouts on your work team will fall somewhere in the northeast quadrant of the matrix. Those who are willing but unable will appear someplace in the northwest, those who are unwilling but able in the southeast, and those who are unwilling and unable in the southwest.

The completed matrix, with all of your work group scored and plotted, provides a wonderful blueprint for human capital development. Now it's possible to develop a plan for each individual depending on where they fall. Your plan will be different for each person. Instead of "one size fits all" human capital development, you'll engage in one-on-one, "one size fits one" human capital development, which is your most important job.

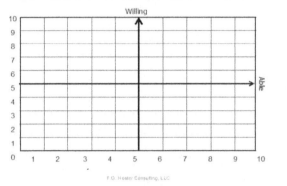

Figure 1

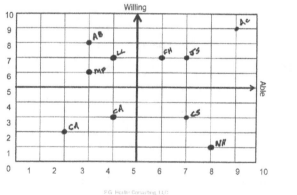

Figure 2

Of course, your true standouts appear in the northeast quadrant (willing and able), and within that quadrant, some will be more northeast than others.

People who are in the northwest quadrant (willing but unable) may be new to the organization (still in training), someone who was recently moved to a new role (still learning a new job), or someone who has been placed in a role that they are not well suited for.

People in the two north quadrants are the strength and potential strength of your group. They are the ones you should be investing in most heavily. To "bring home the pennant," you need a work group, of whom 100 percent score above the horizontal axis and, in fact, are already in the northeast quadrant or can move there quickly.

Southwest quadrant individuals are those who are, in most ways, unwilling and unable. There are a variety of reasons why people wind up in this quadrant. While a few can be successfully moved above the horizontal axis, most can't. These individuals represent a huge drag to your work group or team. If your valued northeast quadrant players dislike anything at all about your leadership, it's most likely that they have to carry the weight for these individuals, and you allow it to continue. If these valued northeast quadrant players decide to leave your team, it just might be for this reason.

Southeast quadrant players are those individuals who are able to perform their jobs very well. Sometimes, technically speaking, they are your best, but they are unwilling to engage in needed behaviors and/or unwilling to avoid other behaviors. An example might be a long-tenured, knowledgeable, technically competent member of your work group who mistreats others, engages in gossip, and seeds discontent.

How do you move people on the matrix? The answer is simply stated but not simply done. It's hard work, and for your direct reports, only you can do it. The good news is that, while it takes a lot of time and effort, it's the highest return-on-investment work you can engage in. Leaders who do this well "win pennants." Those who don't, don't.

Here's how you'll work the plan:

For those appearing in the northwest quadrant (willing but unable), you'll engage in one-on-one coaching that is focused on assessing needs, arranging training, evaluating their response to training, and helping them to develop their skills and their confidence. In doing these things, your objective is to move them to the northeast quadrant (willing and able) as quickly as possible. A tactic you include in your work with them is to partner them with someone who is already in the northeast quadrant (willing and able) who can help them grow and get there.

For those already appearing in the northeast quadrant (willing and able), you need to continue providing coaching support, celebrate their work with them, role-model them, make sure they know they are valued and rewarded, and partner them with northwest quadrant individuals (willing but unable) so that they can help you create the work group of standouts you need, and they want.

For those appearing below the horizontal line, southwest (unwilling and unable) or southeast (unwilling but able), your work is the same. One-on-one coaching that includes a complete assessment of their circumstances and needs. Include in your discussions alignment of objectives. In other words, are their personal professional objectives aligned with those of your work group? Also, evaluate their need for added training. Finally, you should provide them with very clear expectations. Your objective in doing this work is to move them above the horizontal line or, if they cannot be moved, out of the organization. How long do you give yourself to see the results you want? Three months is generous. If an individual operating below the horizontal line hasn't moved north of that in three months, they probably never will, and you don't have more time. By the way, among those who do respond favorably, those in the southeast quadrant (unwilling but able) will move directly to the northeast quadrant, and those in the southwest (unable and unwilling) will move directly to the northwest (willing but unable), making it possible, through continued work with them, as described for the northwest quadrant (willing but unable) players above, to move them to the northeast (willing and able).

An executive summary of the work above is as follows:

Northwest quadrant (willing but unable): coaching, assessment, training, evaluation, development. (Move to NE [willing and able]/partner with NE [willing and able].)

Northeast quadrant (willing and able): coach, reward, support, celebrate, role-model, and develop. (Partner with NW [willing but unable].)

Southwest quadrant (unwilling and unable): coaching, assessment/evaluation, training, alignment of objectives, clear expectations. (Move to NW [willing but unable] and then to NE [willing and able] or out.)

Southeast quadrant (unwilling but able): coaching, assessment/evaluation, alignment of objectives, clear expectations. (Move to NE [willing and able] or out.)

Some really important caveats:

1. While it's challenging, it's critically important that you score yourself first. Be brutally honest with yourself to see where you fall on the matrix. If you are not in the northeast quadrant (willing and able), stop. Do not continue the exercise. Through introspection, and with help from your boss, determine what the two of you need to do to get you there. If you don't think you can get there, or you don't want to get there, you're in the wrong job.

2. This *is not* a tool that you place on the staff bulletin board or share with others. Resist the temptation to show it to individuals as you counsel. It's simply a private tool you use that helps you achieve some measure of objectivity regarding each individual on your team and helps you prepare yourself to be an effective coach for each member of your team. It will also help you track progress by rescoring individuals over time as you engage in that development work with them. When you are sure that everyone who reports to you is operating in the NE quadrant, teach all of this to them so that they can use it with their teams, and so on, through the entire organization.

The "willing and able" method of human capital management is a powerful tool that can, used properly, help you build the team you'll need to bring home the pennant. Of course, used improperly, it can be damaging.

Remember, in any endeavor, successful human capital management is the driving force behind sustained competitiveness. *This is the most important work you will do. If you do nothing else but get this right, you'll succeed as a leader. If you don't do this well, no matter what else you do or how hard you try, you are destined to mediocrity or failure.*

Just think for a moment about the difference in performance between the team represented in figure 3 below versus the team represented in figure 4, and even figure 5 below. If you inherit the team in figure 3 and turn it into the team represented in figure 4, your team's overall performance will improve dramatically. People will notice, and you will deserve to be proud. If you turn it into the team represented in figure 5, it *will* become the stuff of legends.

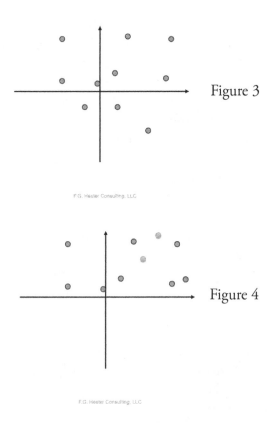

Figure 3

F.G. Hester Consulting, LLC

Figure 4

F.G. Hester Consulting, LLC

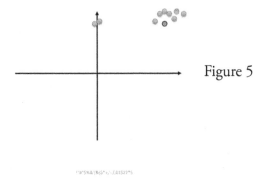

Figure 5

To organizations whose competitive advantage lies in people, recruiting, developing, and retaining talent is not something leaders ought to do when they have some free time. It is the heart of a leader's job. (Jack Welch, former CEO of General Electric)

Epilogue

By every measure, my professional and my personal life have been blessed. My wife Lou and I, now married 52 years, raised four wonderful children who are all successful leaders in their own lives. It was my honor to serve my country, and I was privileged to serve in several roles of increasing responsibility in one of this nation's leading health systems.

Throughout my professional journey, the quotes, phrases and ideas that made their way to my bulletin board, then into who and what I am, were critical in my life and my work.

Far more important than personal and professional success, the wisdom in those ideas, put into daily practice, allowed me to contribute to significant work that helped others.

But, this is where my story ends. The most important story now is your story.

How will you lead?

What timeless leadership truths will you put on your wall and live out?

What will you and those around you accomplish together?

What will be your legacy?

It's really up to you, and I think that's the most wonderful and exciting part.

I wish you and those around you all the best in life and in work.

> The person who is truly effective has the humility and reverence to recognize his own perceptual limitations and to appreciate the rich resources available through interactions with the hearts and minds of other human beings. —Stephen Covey

About the Author

Prior to his full retirement in 2015, Woody served as principal of his own consulting company for five years, convening and facilitating a leadership learning forum for company CEOs as well as one for COOs. That was immediately preceded by thirty-eight years in the health-care industry, during which he served in various capacities, including health system senior vice president and chief people officer, president and chief executive officer of a community hospital, and vice president of operations for a large teaching hospital, where he also served as assistant vice president of administrative services, administrator of operations development, and director of pharmacy. Woody holds a BS in pharmacy from Ferris State University and an MA in communication from the University of Illinois Springfield. He also completed a clinical pharmacy clerkship at the University of Illinois Hospital, Chicago, as well as a postgraduate fellowship at the University of Pennsylvania's Leonard Davis Institute. Woody was a fellow (retired) in the American College of Healthcare Executives (FACHE—retired), was board-certified in health-care management, and was a credentialed senior professional in human resources (SPHR—retired). Woody served in the US Army from 1967 to 1971, attained the rank of captain, and was awarded a Bronze Star and Bronze Star with Oak Leaf Cluster, serving as an air observer and a field artillery service battery commander in the Republic of South Vietnam. Woody has been married to Louise Lambert Hester for fifty-two years. They have four grown children and eleven grandchildren.

CPSIA information can be obtained
at www.ICGtesting.com
Printed in the USA
LVHW090105300921
699111LV00001B/1

9 781636 305929